------- Innus Art -------

Alphabet A

Color the picture and trace the word

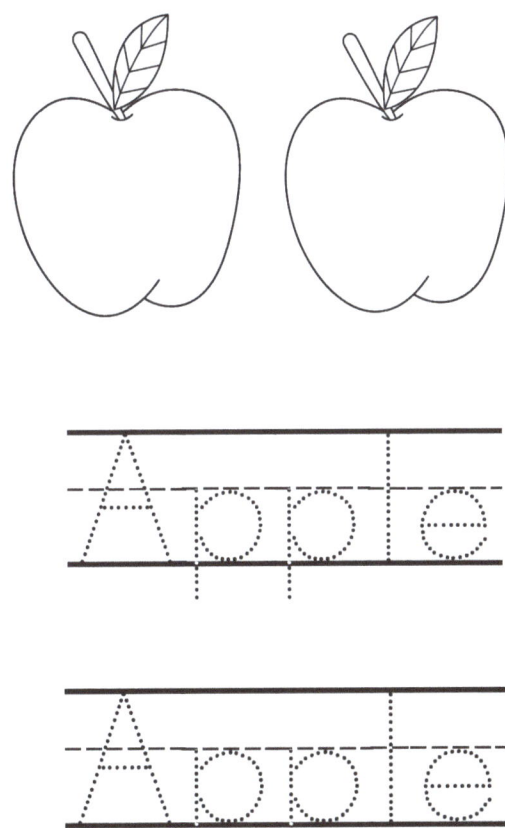

- - - - - - - - - Innus Art - - - - - - - -

Alphabet B

Color the picture and trace the word

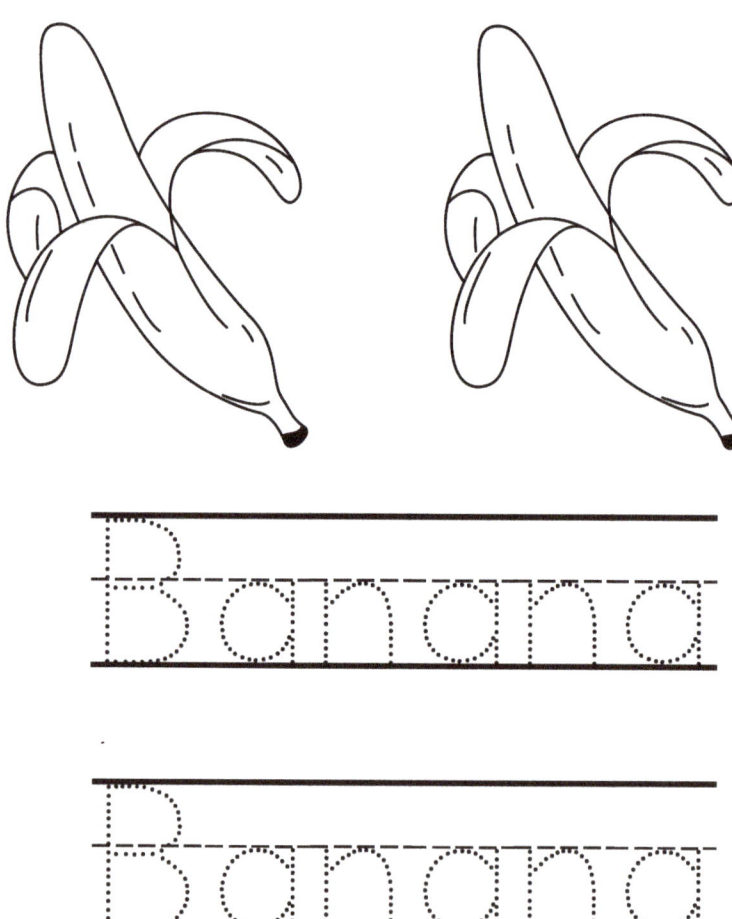

- - - - - - - - Innu Arts - - - - - - - -

Alphabet C

Color the picture and trace the word

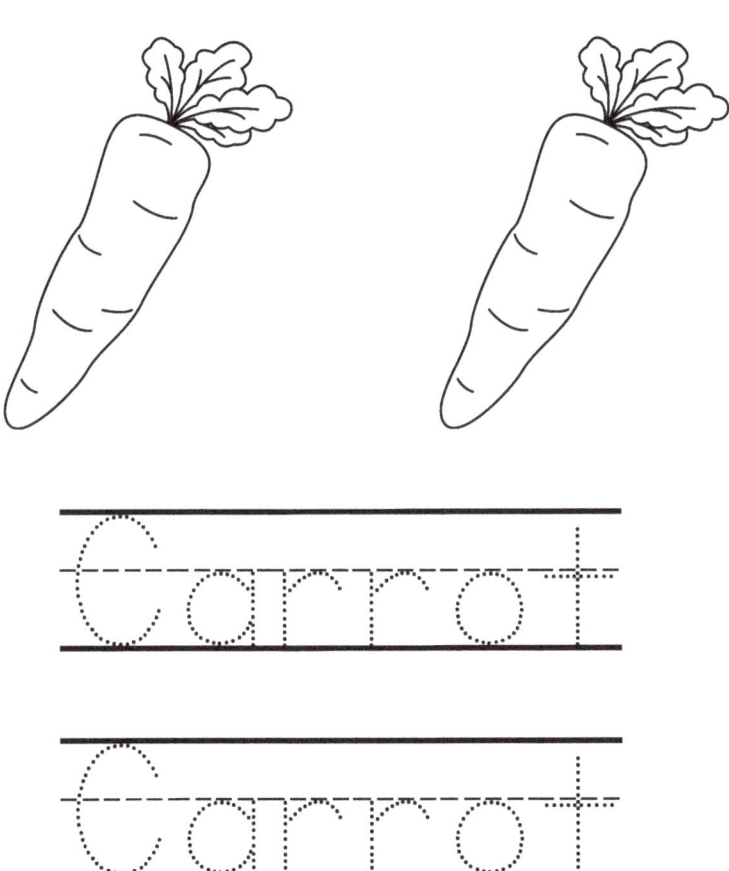

------------- Innus Art -------------

Alphabet D

Color the picture and trace the word

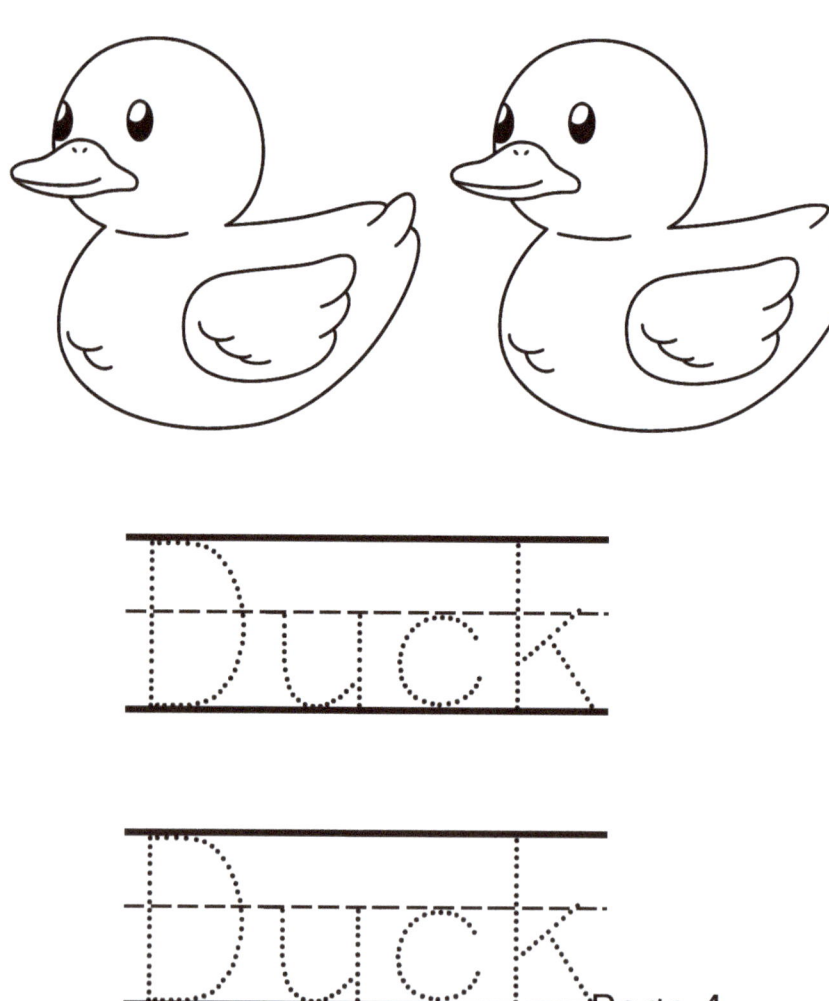

■ ■ ■ ■ ■ ■ ■ ■ ■ Innus Art ■ ■ ■ ■ ■ ■ ■ ■ ■

Alphabet E

Color the picture and trace the word

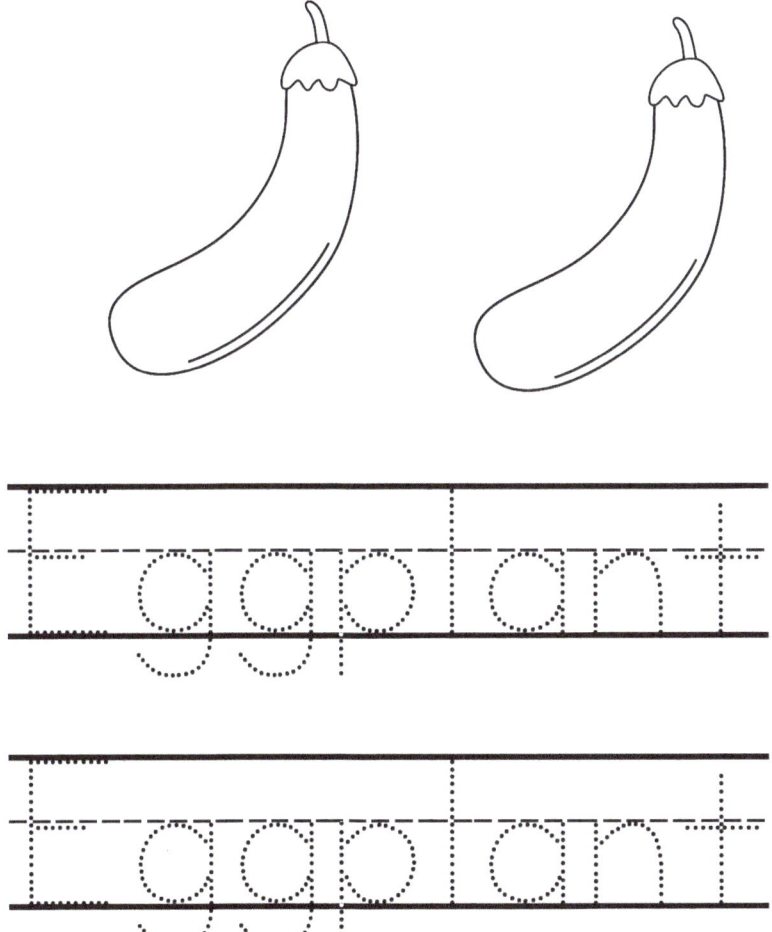

Eggplant

Eggplant

Alphabet F

Color the picture and trace the word

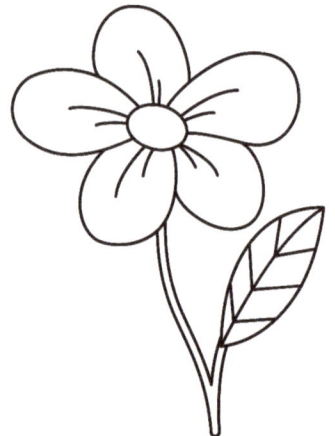
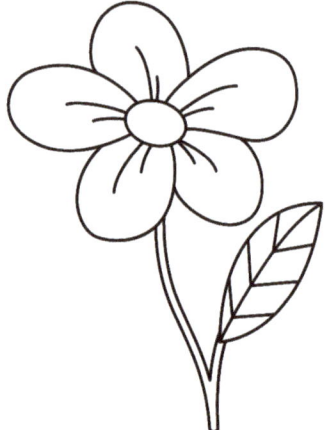

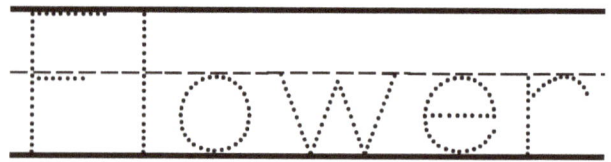

---------- Innus Art ----------

Alphabet G

Color the picture and trace the word

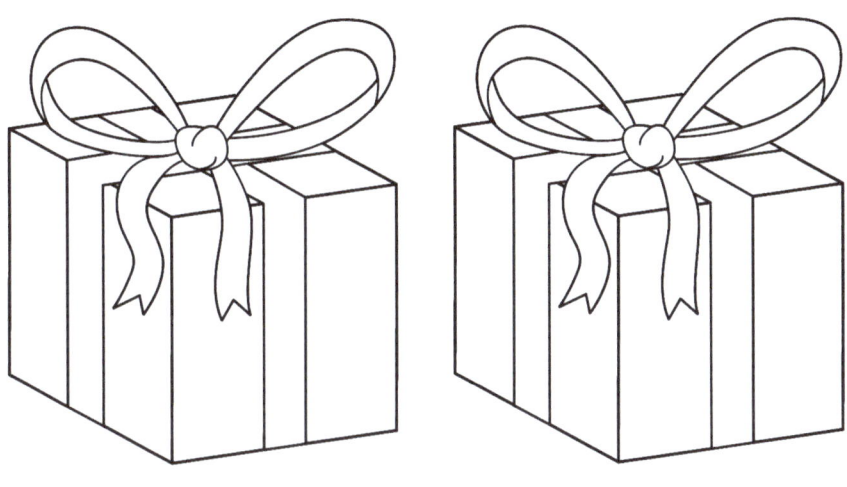

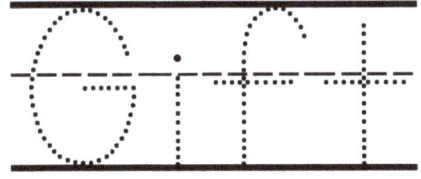

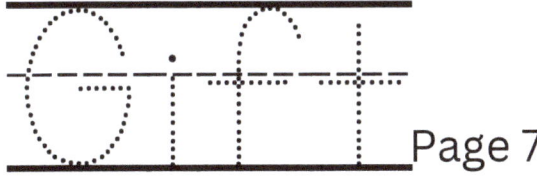

---------- Innus Art ----------

Alphabet H

Color the picture and trace the word

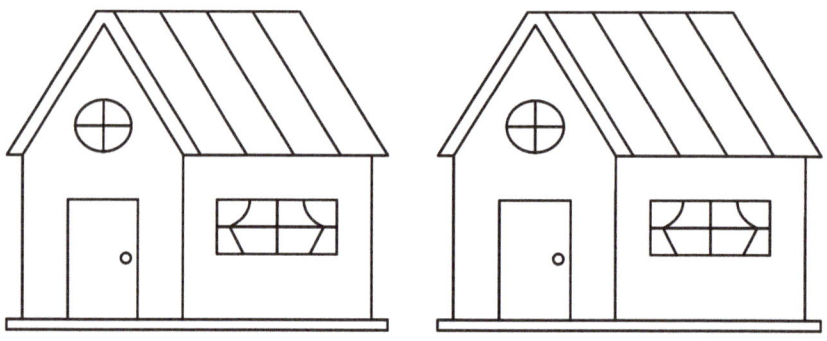

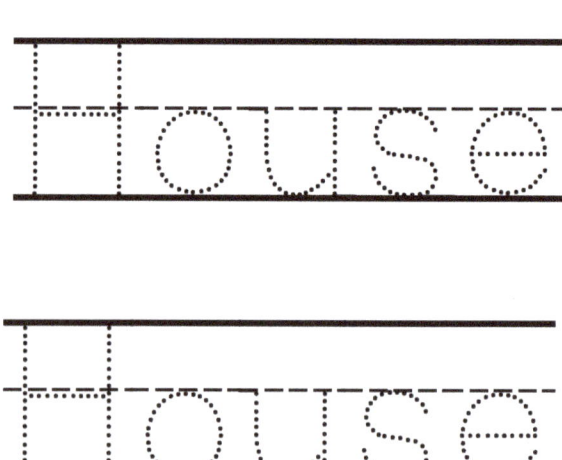

Alphabet I

Color the picture and trace the word

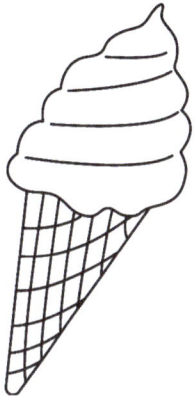 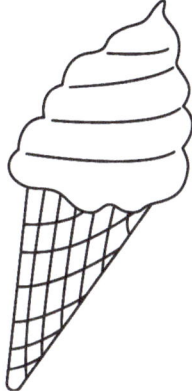

Ice Cream

Ice Cream

––––––––– Innus Art –––––––––

Alphabet J

Color the picture and trace the word

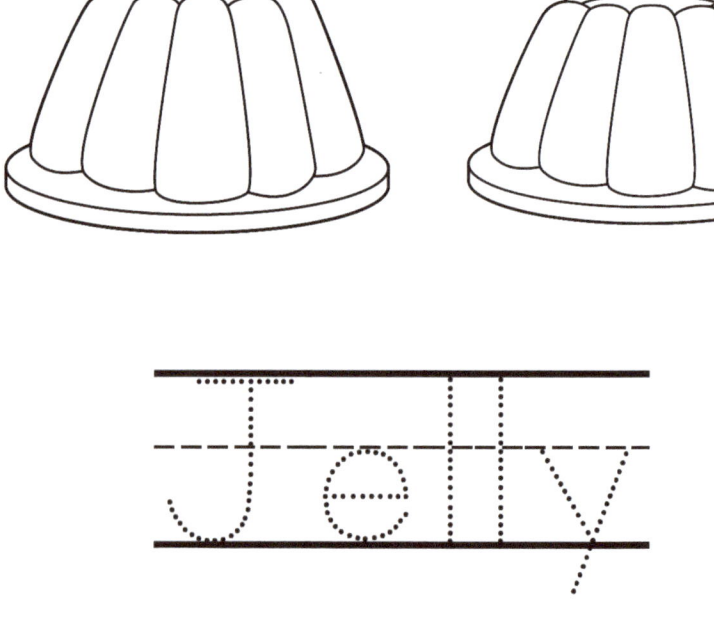

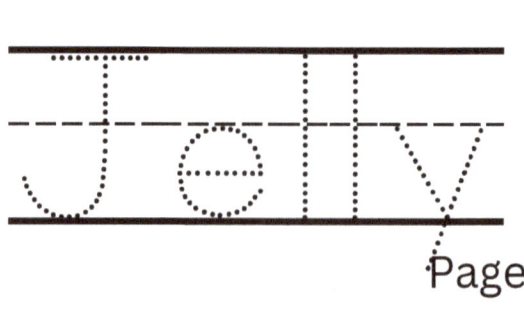

Alphabet K

Color the picture and trace the word

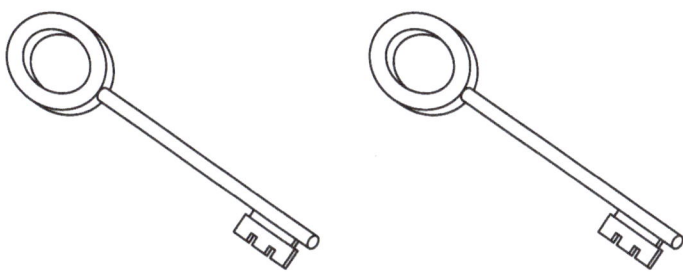

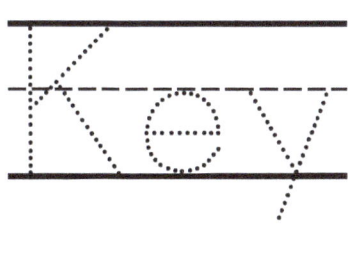

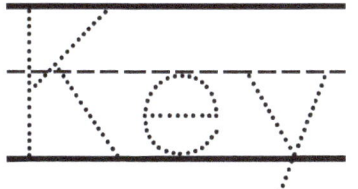

Alphabet L

Color the picture and trace the word

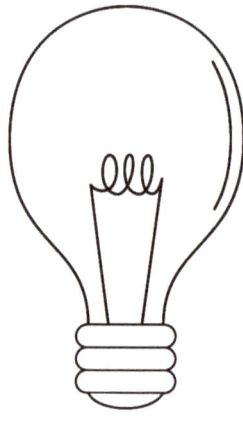
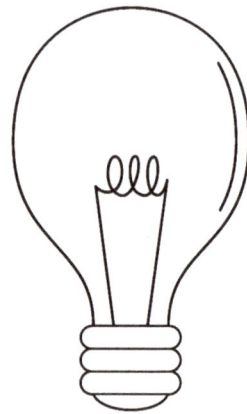

Light Bulb

Light Bulb

Alphabet M

Color the picture and trace the word

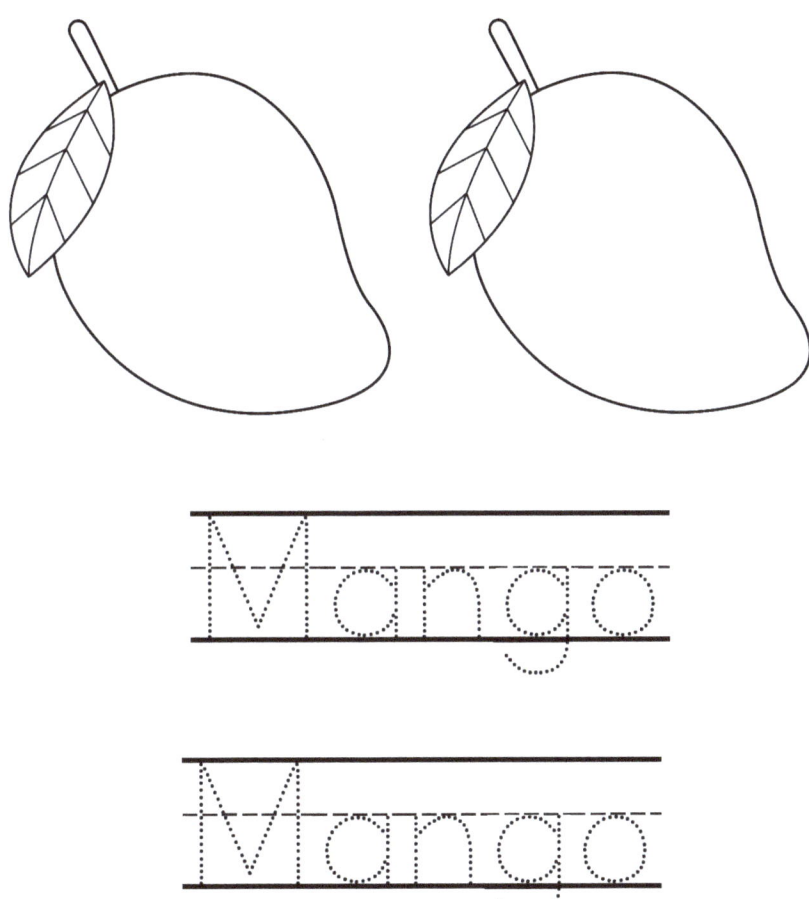

Alphabet N

Color the picture and trace the word

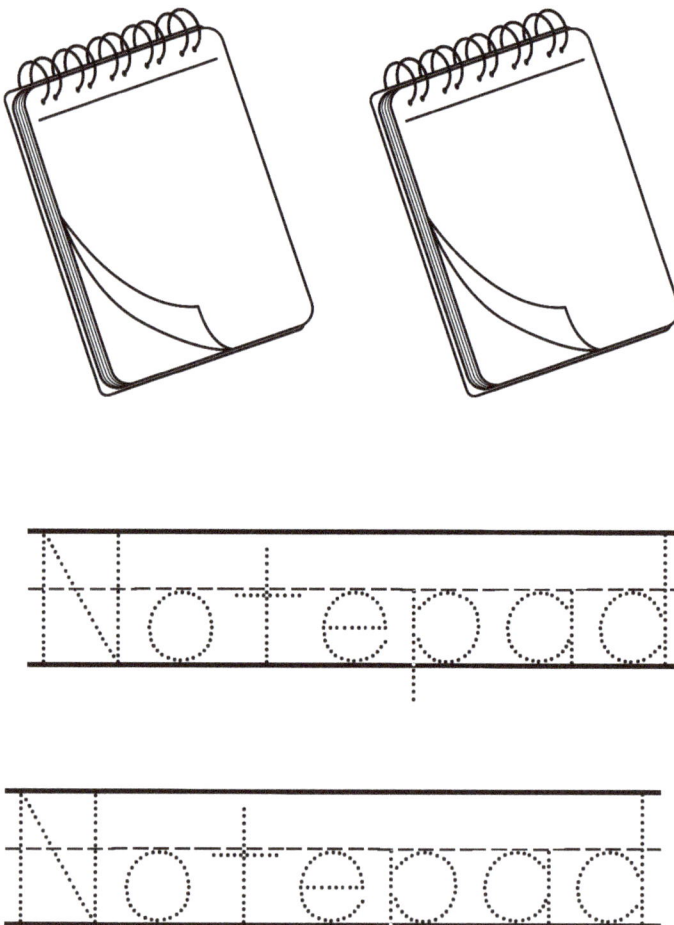

Notepad

Notepad

Alphabet O

Color the picture and trace the word

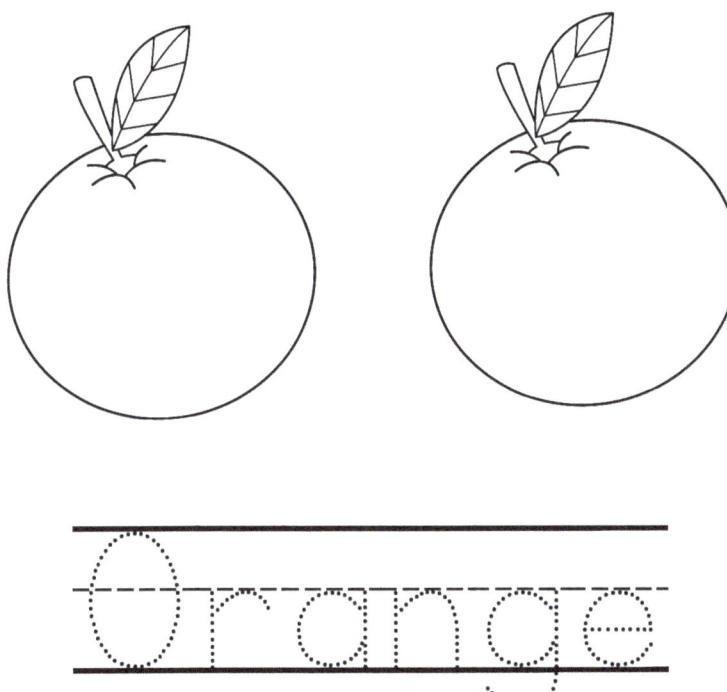

Alphabet P

Color the picture and trace the word

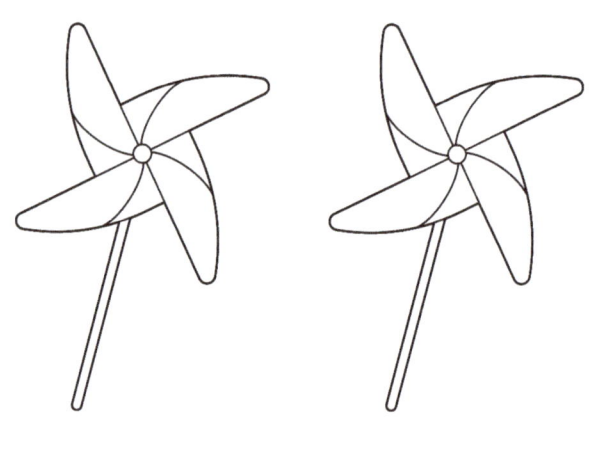

Pinwheel

Pinwheel

Alphabet Q

Color the picture and trace the word

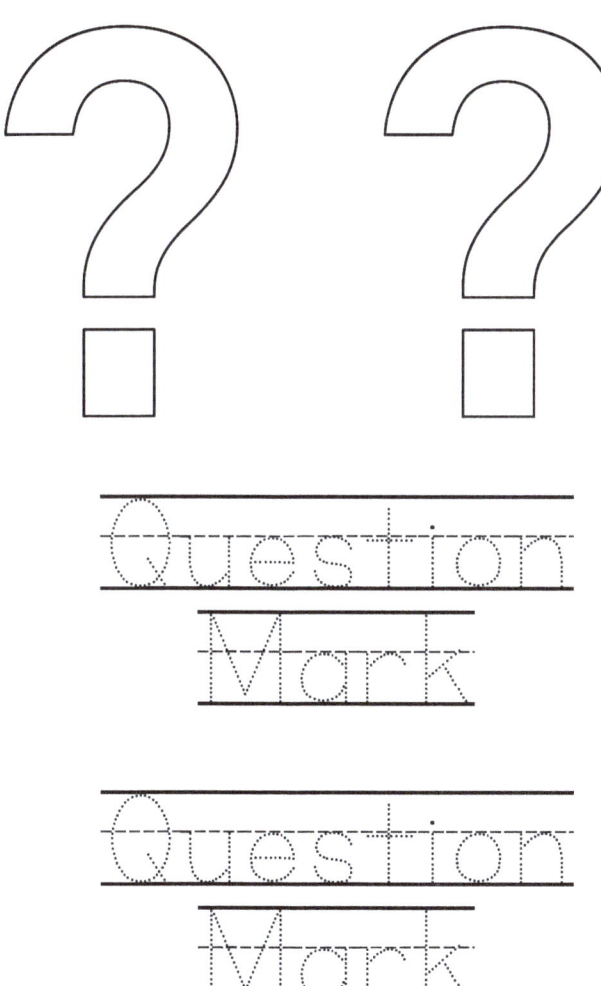

---- Innus Art ----

Alphabet R

Color the picture and trace the word

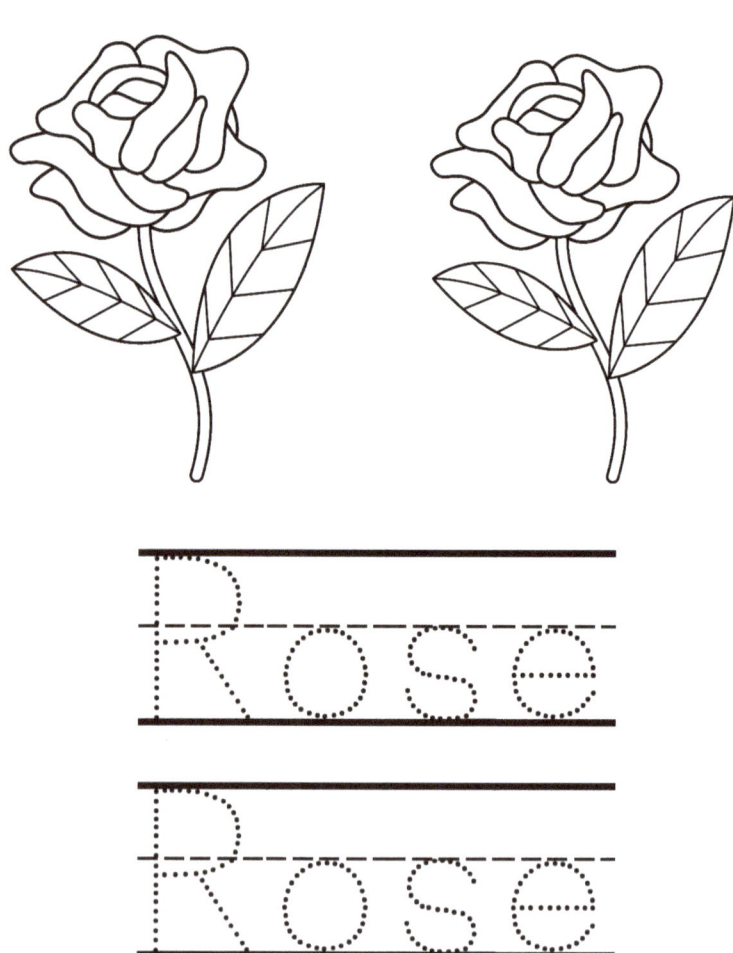

Alphabet S

Color the picture and trace the word

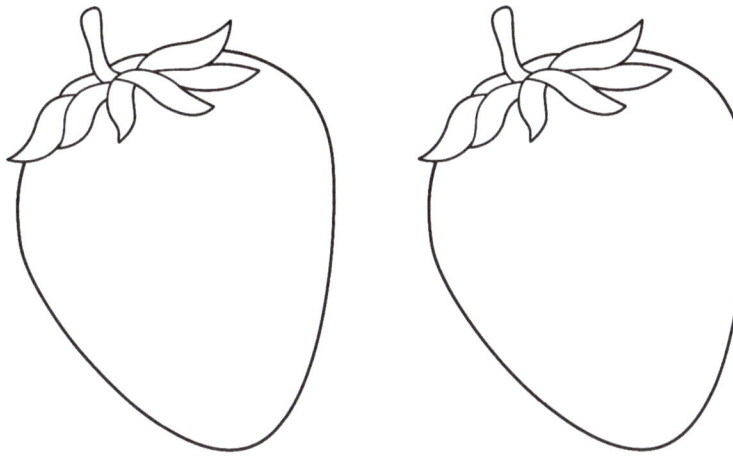

Strawberry

Strawberry

--------- Innus Art ---------

Alphabet T

Color the picture and trace the word

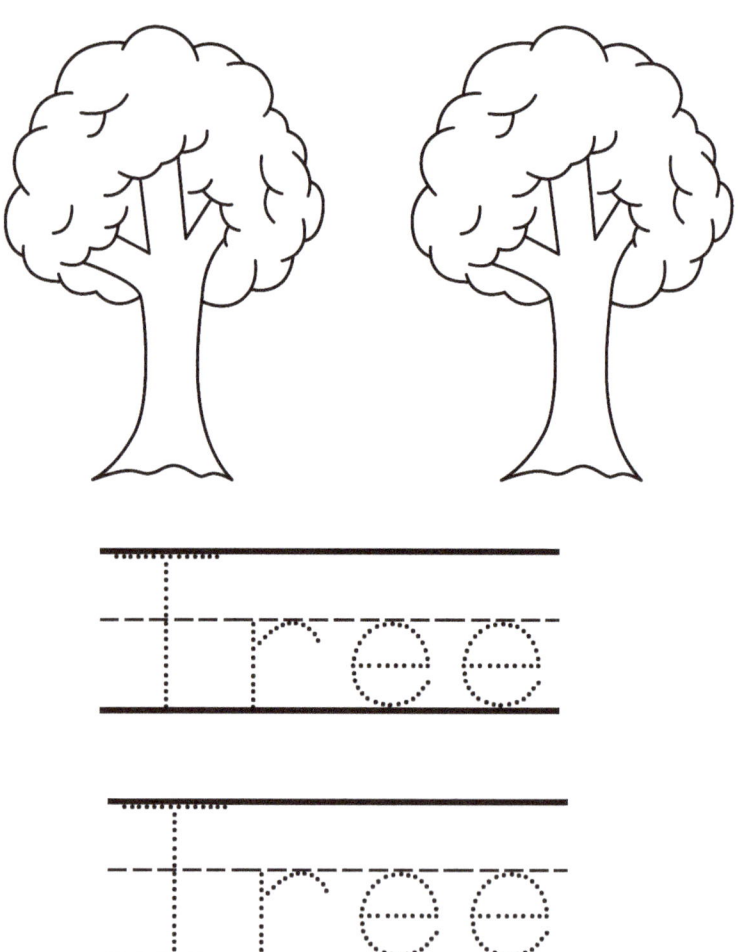

Page 20

---------- Innus Art ----------

Alphabet U

Color the picture and trace the word

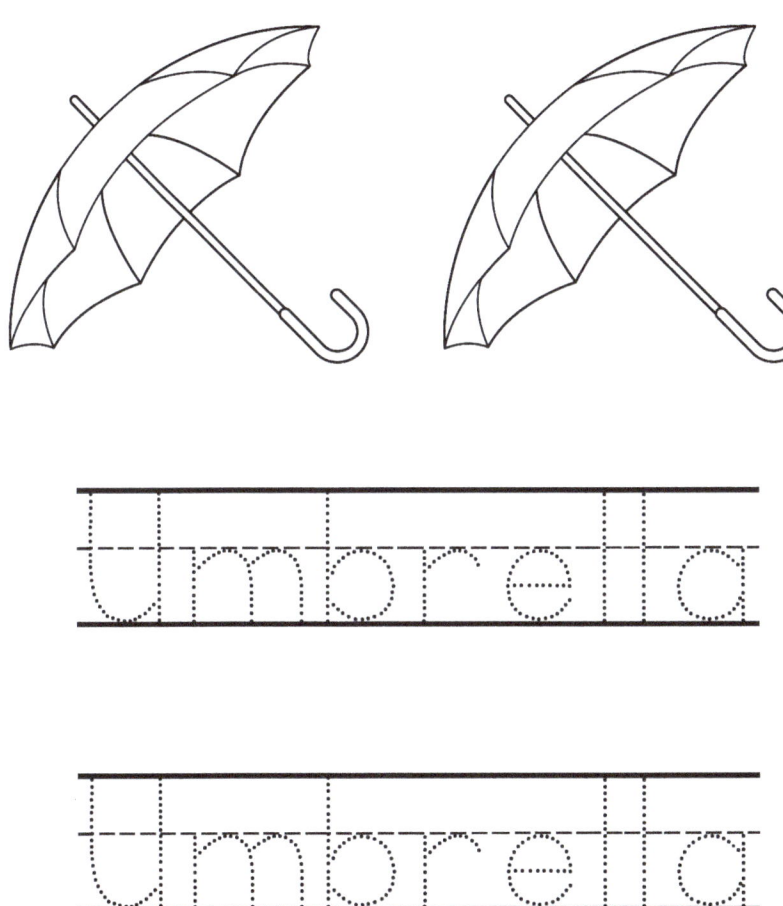

Umbrella

Umbrella

---------- Innus Art ----------

Alphabet V

Color the picture and trace the word

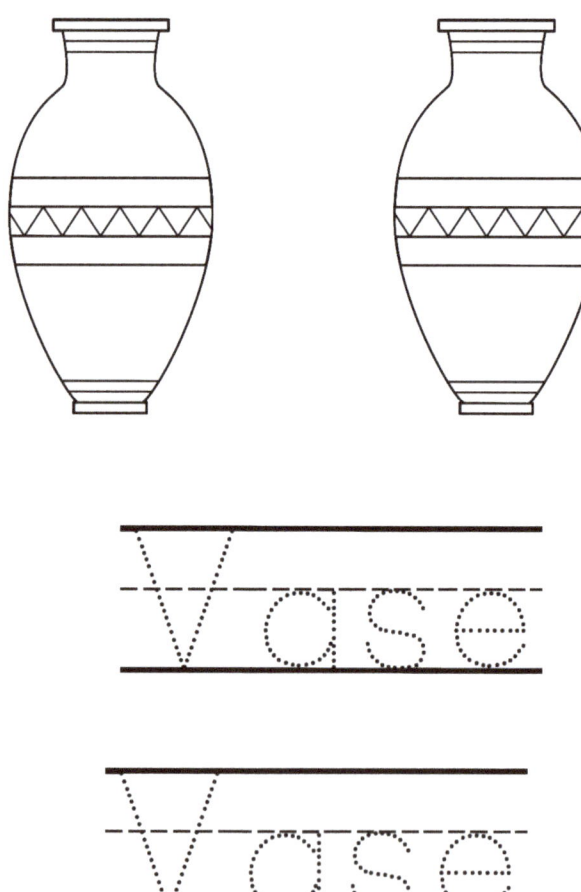

Vase

Vase

------------- Innus Art -------------

Alphabet W

Color the picture and trace the word

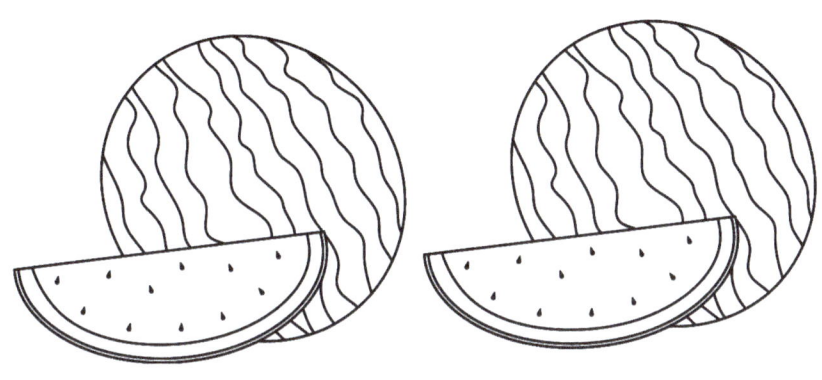

Watermelon

Watermelon

---------- Innus Art ----------

Alphabet X

Color the picture and trace the word

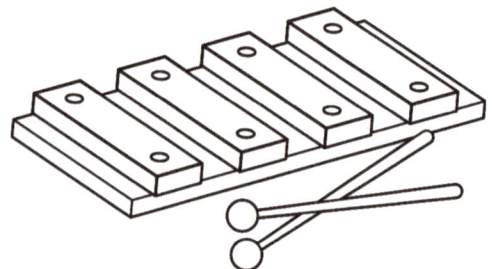

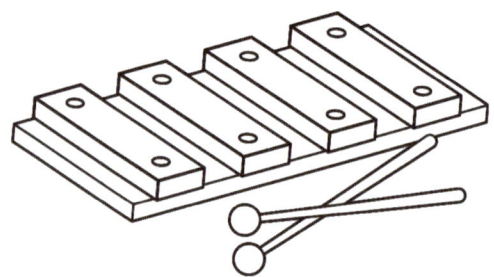

Xylophone

──────── Innus Art ────────

Alphabet y

Color the picture and trace the word

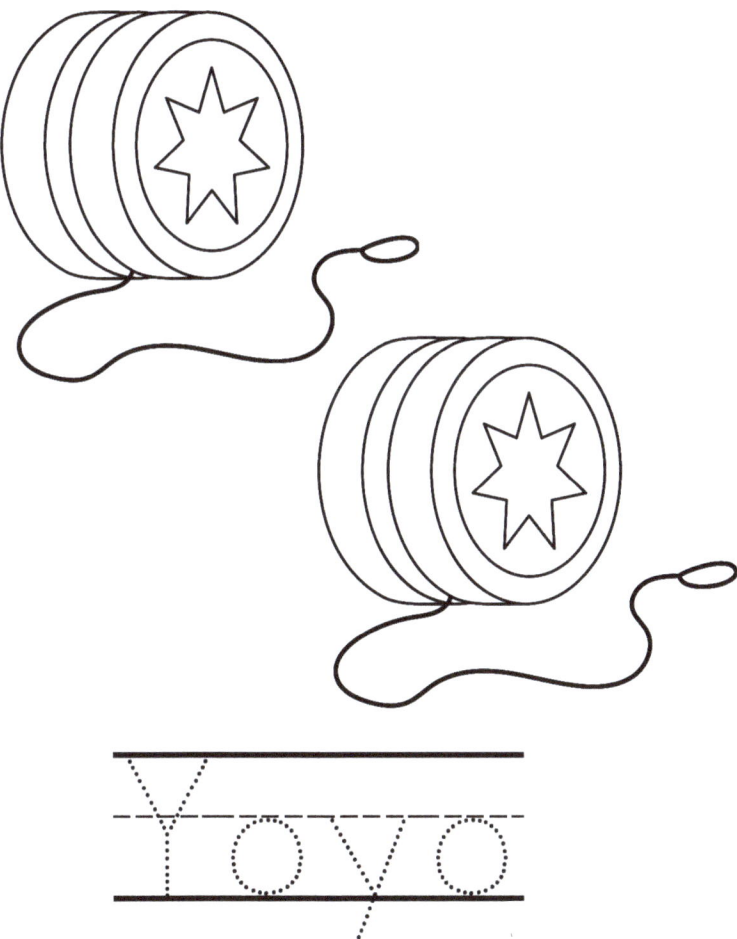

Yoyo

Innus Art

Alphabet Z

Color the picture and trace the word

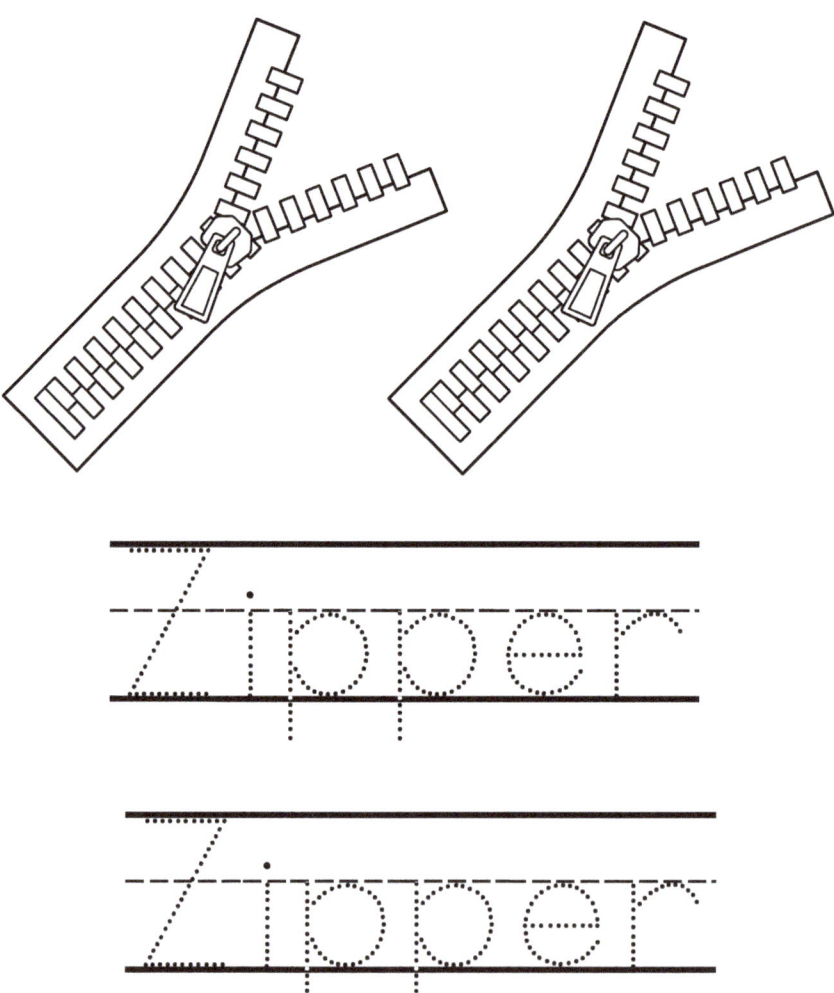

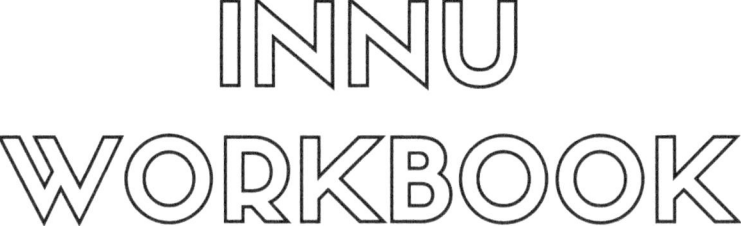

www.ingramcontent.com/pod-product-compliance
Lightning Source LLC
Chambersburg PA
CBHW040349220526
45473CB00009B/2825